APR 30 2010

THE NURSERY RHYME BOOK

Illustrated by Anne Anderson
and Lisa Jackson

Compiled by Helen Cumberbatch

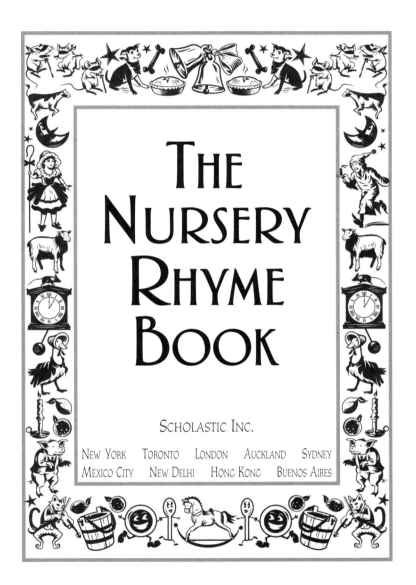

THE
NURSERY
RHYME
BOOK

SCHOLASTIC INC.

NEW YORK   TORONTO   LONDON   AUCKLAND   SYDNEY
MEXICO CITY   NEW DELHI   HONG KONG   BUENOS AIRES

Library of Congress Cataloging-in-Publication data is available.

ISBN-13: 978-0-545-13404-0
ISBN-10: 0-545-13404-8

First published in Great Britain in 2008 by Michael O'Mara Books Limited,
9 Lion Yard, Tremadoc Road, London SW4 7NQ
www.mombooks.com

12 11 10 9 8 7 6 5 4 3 2 1   9 10 11 12 13 14/0

Printed in the U.S.A.
First American edition, August 2009

CONTENTS

About the Illustrators

Anne Anderson (1874–1930) spent much of her childhood in Argentina. In 1912, she married the painter Alan Wright, and they worked on several children's books together.

Anne became a hugely popular illustrator. She worked in watercolor and in black-and-white line art. Her pictures in this book are taken from *Old English Nursery Songs*.

Lisa Jackson was born in Dublin and grew up in County Wicklow, Ireland. She studied classical animation and then went on to work in graphic design and comic books.

Lisa now concentrates on children's book illustration, creating her work with a mix of traditional and digital media. She currently lives in Dublin, Ireland.

Introduction

The long-established tradition of reading or singing nursery rhymes to young children is a delightful pastime. It has also been proven to help children develop their language and reading ability, as well as their memory, vocabulary, and communication skills.

Mary, Mary, Quite Contrary

Mary, Mary, quite contrary,
How does your garden grow?
With silver bells and cockleshells,
And pretty maids all in a row.

Bobby Shafto

Bobby Shafto's gone to sea,
Silver buckles on his knee;
He'll come back and marry me,
Bonny Bobby Shafto!

Bobby Shafto's fat and fair,
Combing down his yellow hair;
He's my love forevermore,
Bonny Bobby Shafto!

Lucy Locket

Lucy Locket lost her pocket,
Kitty Fisher found it;
Not a penny was there in it,
Only ribbon 'round it.

Rain, Rain, Go Away

Rain, rain, go away,
Come again another day.

Rain, rain, go to Spain,
Never show your face again!

Humpty Dumpty

Humpty Dumpty sat on a wall,
Humpty Dumpty had a great fall.
All the king's horses,
And all the king's men,
Couldn't put Humpty together again.

Little Bo-Peep

Little Bo-Peep has lost her sheep,
And doesn't know where to find them;
Leave them alone, and they'll come home,
Bringing their tails behind them.

Little Bo-Peep fell fast asleep,
And dreamed she heard them bleating;
But when she awoke, she found it a joke,
For they were still all fleeting.

Then up she took her little crook,
Determined for to find them;
She found them indeed, but it made her heart bleed,
For they'd left their tails behind them.

It happened one day, as Bo-Peep did stray
Into a meadow hard by,
There she espied their tails side by side
All hung on a tree to dry.

She heaved a sigh, and wiped her eye,
And over the hillocks went rambling,
And tried what she could, as a shepherdess should,
To tack again each to its lambkin.

Pop Goes the Weasel

All around the mulberry bush,
The monkey chased the weasel;
The monkey thought 'twas all in fun.
Pop goes the weasel!

A penny for a spool of thread,
A penny for a needle;
That's the way the money goes,
Pop goes the weasel!

The Grand Old Duke of York

Oh, the grand old Duke of York,
He had ten thousand men;
He marched them up to the top of the hill,
And he marched them down again.

And when they were up, they were up,
And when they were down, they were down,
And when they were only halfway up
They were neither up nor down.

Ladybird, Ladybird

Ladybird, ladybird,
Fly away home,
Your house is on fire,
And your children all gone.

All except one,
And that's little Ann,
And she has crept under
The frying pan.

Rock-A-Bye, Baby

Rock-a-bye, baby, on the treetop,
When the wind blows, the cradle will rock;
When the bough breaks, the cradle will fall,
And down will come baby, cradle and all.

Aiken Drum

There was a man who lived in the moon,
lived in the moon, lived in the moon.
There was a man who lived in the moon,
And his name was Aiken Drum.

Chorus:
And he played upon a ladle, a ladle, a ladle,
And he played upon a ladle,
And his name was Aiken Drum.

And his hat was made of good cream cheese,
of good cream cheese, of good cream cheese.
And his hat was made of good cream cheese,
And his name was Aiken Drum.

Chorus

And his coat was made of good roast beef,
of good roast beef, of good roast beef.
And his coat was made of good roast beef,
And his name was Aiken Drum.

Chorus

And his buttons were made of penny loaves,
of penny loaves, of penny loaves.
And his buttons were made of penny loaves,
And his name was Aiken Drum.

Chorus

And his breeches were made of haggis bags,
of haggis bags, of haggis bags.
And his breeches were made of haggis bags,
And his name was Aiken Drum.

Hey, Diddle, Diddle

Hey, diddle, diddle,
The cat and the fiddle,
The cow jumped over the moon;
The little dog laughed
To see such fun,
And the dish ran away with the spoon.

Old Mother Hubbard

Old Mother Hubbard
Went to the cupboard,
To get her poor dog a bone;
But when she got there,
The cupboard was bare,
And so the poor dog had none.

Jack Sprat

Jack Sprat could eat no fat,
His wife could eat no lean,
And so betwixt the two of them
They licked the platter clean.

Jack ate all the lean,
Joan ate all the fat.
The bone they picked it clean,
Then gave it to the cat.

Jack Sprat was wheeling
His wife by the ditch.
The barrow turned over,
And in she did pitch.

Says Jack, "She'll be drowned!"
But Joan did reply,
"I don't think I shall,
For the ditch is quite dry."

London Bridge Is Falling Down

London Bridge is falling down,
Falling down, falling down,
London Bridge is falling down,
My fair lady.

Build it up with wood and clay,
Wood and clay, wood and clay,
Build it up with wood and clay,
My fair lady.

Wood and clay will wash away,
Wash away, wash away,
Wood and clay will wash away,
My fair lady.

Build it up with bricks and mortar,
Bricks and mortar, bricks and mortar,
Build it up with bricks and mortar,
My fair lady.

Bricks and mortar will not stay,
Will not stay, will not stay,
Bricks and mortar will not stay,
My fair lady.

Build it up with iron and steel,
Iron and steel, iron and steel,
Build it up with iron and steel,
My fair lady.

Iron and steel will bend and bow,
Bend and bow, bend and bow,
Iron and steel will bend and bow,
My fair lady.

Build it up with silver and gold,
Silver and gold, silver and gold,
Build it up with silver and gold,
My fair lady.

Silver and gold will be stolen away,
Stolen away, stolen away,
Silver and gold will be stolen away,
My fair lady.

Set a man to watch all night,
Watch all night, watch all night,
Set a man to watch all night,
My fair lady.

Suppose the man should fall asleep,
Fall asleep, fall asleep,
Suppose the man should fall asleep,
My fair lady.

Give him a pipe to smoke all night,
Smoke all night, smoke all night,
Give him a pipe to smoke all night,
My fair lady.

For Want of a Nail

For want of a nail, the shoe was lost,
For want of a shoe, the horse was lost,
For want of a horse, the rider was lost,
For want of a rider, the battle was lost,
For want of a battle, the kingdom was lost,
And all for the want of a horseshoe nail.

Cock-A-Doodle-Doo!

Cock-a-doodle-doo!
My dame has lost her shoe,
My master's lost his fiddling stick,
And knows not what to do.

Cock-a-doodle-doo!
What is my dame to do?
Till master finds his fiddling stick,
She'll dance without her shoe.

Cock-a-doodle-doo!
My dame has found her shoe,
And master's found his fiddling stick,
Sing doodle-doodle-doo.

Cock-a-doodle-doo!
My dame will dance with you,
While master fiddles his fiddling stick,
For dame and doodle-doo.

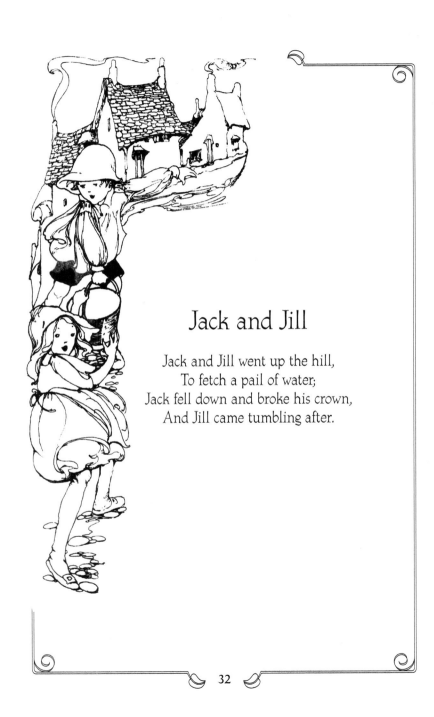

Jack and Jill

Jack and Jill went up the hill,
To fetch a pail of water;
Jack fell down and broke his crown,
And Jill came tumbling after.

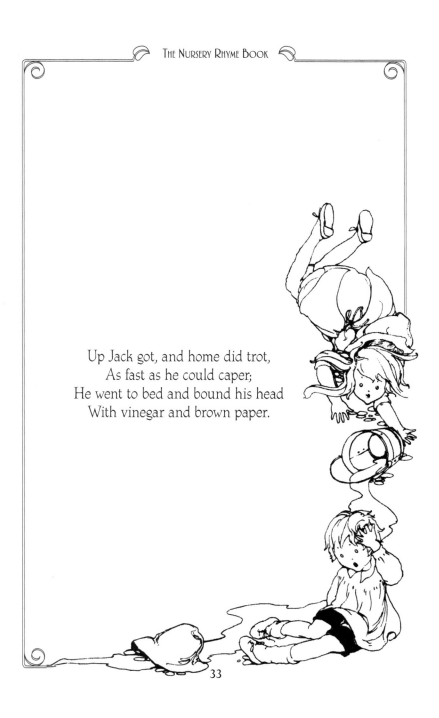

Up Jack got, and home did trot,
As fast as he could caper;
He went to bed and bound his head
With vinegar and brown paper.

The Big Ship Sails on the Ally-Ally-Oh

The big ship sails on the ally-ally-oh, the ally-ally-oh,
the ally-ally-oh.
Oh, the big ship sails on the ally-ally-oh,
on the last day of September.

The captain said it will never, never do,
never, never do, never, never do.
The captain said it will never, never do,
on the last day of September.

We all dip our heads in the deep blue sea,
the deep blue sea, the deep blue sea.
We all dip our heads in the deep blue sea,
on the last day of September.

The big ship sank to the bottom of the sea,
the bottom of the sea, the bottom of the sea.
The big ship sank to the bottom of the sea,
on the last day of September.

A Wise Old Owl

A wise old owl lived in an oak;
The more he saw, the less he spoke;
The less he spoke, the more he heard.
Why can't we all be like that wise old bird?

Old King Cole

Old King Cole
Was a merry old soul,
And a merry old soul was he;
He called for his pipe,
And he called for his bowl,
And he called for his fiddlers three.

Every fiddler, he had a fiddle,
And a very fine fiddle had he;
Oh, there's none so rare
As can compare
With King Cole and his fiddlers three.

The Queen of Hearts

The Queen of Hearts
She made some tarts,
All on a summer's day;
The Knave of Hearts
He stole the tarts,
And took them clean away.

The King of Hearts
Called for the tarts,
And beat the Knave full sore;
The Knave of Hearts
Brought back the tarts,
And vowed he'd steal no more.

As I Was Going to St. Ives

As I was going to St. Ives,
I met a man with seven wives.
Each wife had seven sacks,
Each sack had seven cats,
Each cat had seven kits.
Kits, cats, sacks, and wives,
How many were going to St. Ives?

Pease Porridge Hot

Pease porridge hot,
Pease porridge cold,
Pease porridge in the pot,
Nine days old.

Some like it hot,
Some like it cold,
Some like it in the pot,
Nine days old.

Sing a Song of Sixpence

Sing a song of sixpence, a pocket full of rye;
Four and twenty blackbirds baked in a pie.
When the pie was opened, the birds began to sing.
Oh, wasn't that a dainty dish to set before the king?

The king was in his countinghouse, counting out his money;
The queen was in the parlor, eating bread and honey.
The maid was in the garden, hanging out the clothes,
When down came a blackbird and pecked off her nose.

What Are
Little Boys Made Of?

What are little boys made of?
Frogs and snails, and puppy dogs' tails,
That's what little boys are made of!

What are little girls made of?
Sugar and spice and all things nice,
That's what little girls are made of!

The Itsy-Bitsy Spider

The itsy-bitsy spider climbed up the water spout;
Down came the rain and washed the spider out.
Out came the sun and dried up all the rain;
And the itsy-bitsy spider went up the spout again!

Who Killed Cock Robin?

"Who killed Cock Robin?"
"I," said the Sparrow,
"With my bow and arrow, I killed Cock Robin."
"Who saw him die?"
"I," said the Fly,
"With my little eye, I saw him die."
"Who caught his blood?"
"I," said the Fish,
"With my little dish, I caught his blood."
"Who'll make the shroud?"
"I," said the Beetle,
"With my thread and needle, I'll make the shroud."
"Who'll dig his grave?"
"I," said the Owl,
"With my pick and shovel, I'll dig his grave."
"Who'll be the parson?"
"I," said the Rook,
"With my little book, I'll be the parson."
"Who'll be the clerk?"
"I," said the Lark,
"If it's not in the dark, I'll be the clerk."
"Who'll carry the link?"
"I," said the Linnet,
"I'll fetch it in a minute, I'll carry the link."
"Who'll be chief mourner?"
"I," said the Dove,
"I mourn for my love, I'll be chief mourner."

"Who'll carry the coffin?"
"I," said the Kite,
"If it's not through the night, I'll carry the coffin."
"Who'll bear the pall?"
"We," said the Wren,
"Both the cock and the hen, we'll bear the pall."
"Who'll sing a psalm?"
"I," said the Thrush,
As she sat on a bush, "I'll sing a psalm."
"Who'll toll the bell?"
"I," said the bull,
"Because I can pull, I'll toll the bell."
All the birds of the air fell sighing and sobbing,
When they heard the bell toll for poor
Cock Robin.

Little Polly Flinders

Little Polly Flinders
Sat among the cinders,
Warming her pretty little toes.

Her mother came and caught her,
And whipped her little daughter
For spoiling her nice new clothes.

Hickory, Dickory, Dock

Hickory, dickory, dock,
The mouse ran up the clock.
The clock struck one,
The mouse ran down,
Hickory, dickory, dock.

Seesaw, Margery Daw

Seesaw, Margery Daw,
Johnny shall have a new master.
He shall earn but a penny a day,
Because he can't work any faster.

Star Light, Star Bright

Star light, star bright,
First star I see tonight,
I wish I may, I wish I might,
Have the wish I wish tonight.

The Owl and the Pussycat

The Owl and the Pussycat went to sea
In a beautiful pea-green boat.
They took some honey, and plenty of money,
Wrapped up in a five-pound note.

The Owl looked up to the stars above,
And sang to a small guitar,
"O lovely Pussy! O Pussy, my love,
What a beautiful Pussy you are, you are, you are,
What a beautiful Pussy you are."

Pussy said to the Owl, "You elegant fowl,
How charmingly sweet you sing.
O let us be married, too long we have tarried;
But what shall we do for a ring?"

They sailed away, for a year and a day,
To the land where the Bong-tree grows,
And there in a wood a Piggy-wig stood
With a ring at the end of his nose, his nose, his nose,
With a ring at the end of his nose.

"Dear Pig, are you willing to sell for one
shilling your ring?"
Said the Piggy, "I will."
So they took it away, and were married next day
By the Turkey who lives on the hill.

They dined on mince, and slices of quince,
Which they ate with a runcible spoon.
And hand in hand, on the edge of the sand,
They danced by the light of the moon,
the moon, the moon,
They danced by the light of the moon.

Here We Go 'Round the Mulberry Bush

Here we go 'round the mulberry bush,
The mulberry bush, the mulberry bush.
Here we go 'round the mulberry bush,
So early in the morning.

This is the way we wash our clothes,
Wash our clothes, wash our clothes.
This is the way we wash our clothes,
So early Monday morning.

This is the way we iron our clothes,
Iron our clothes, iron our clothes.
This is the way we iron our clothes,
So early Tuesday morning.

This is the way we mend our clothes,
Mend our clothes, mend our clothes.
This is the way we mend our clothes,
So early Wednesday morning.

This is the way we sweep the house,
Sweep the house, sweep the house.
This is the way we sweep the house,
So early Thursday morning.

This is the way we scrub the floor,
Scrub the floor, scrub the floor.
This is the way we scrub the floor,
So early Friday morning.

This is the way we bake our bread,
Bake our bread, bake our bread.
This is the way we bake our bread,
So early Saturday morning.

This is the way we go to church,
Go to church, go to church.
This is the way we go to church,
So early Sunday morning.

Here we go 'round the mulberry bush,
The mulberry bush, the mulberry bush.
Here we go 'round the mulberry bush,
So early in the morning.

I Had a Little Nut Tree

I had a little nut tree,
Nothing would it bear
But a silver nutmeg
And a golden pear.

The king of Spain's daughter
Came to visit me,
And all for the sake
Of my little nut tree.

I skipped over the water,
I danced over the sea,
And all the birds in the air
Couldn't catch me.

Christmas Is Coming

Christmas is coming,
The geese are getting fat.
Please to put a penny
In the old man's hat.
If you haven't got a penny,
A ha'penny will do;
If you haven't got a ha'penny,
Then God bless you!

Sleep, Baby, Sleep

Sleep, baby, sleep,
Thy papa guards the sheep;
Thy mama shakes the dreamland tree,
And from it fall sweet dreams for thee,
Sleep, baby, sleep.

Sleep, baby, sleep,
Our cottage vale is deep;
The little lamb is on the green,
With woolly fleece so soft and clean,
Sleep, baby, sleep.

Sleep, baby, sleep,
Down where the woodbines creep;
Be always like the lamb so mild,
A kind and sweet and gentle child,
Sleep, baby, sleep.

Baa, Baa, Black Sheep

Baa, baa, black sheep,
Have you any wool?
Yes, sir, yes, sir,
Three bags full!
One for the master,
One for the dame,
And one for the little boy
Who lives down the lane.

Mary Had a Little Lamb

Mary had a little lamb,
Its fleece was white as snow;
And everywhere that Mary went,
The lamb was sure to go.

It followed her to school one day,
Which was against the rule;
It made the children laugh and play
To see a lamb at school.

And so the teacher turned it out,
But still it lingered near,
And waited patiently about
Till Mary did appear.

"Why does the lamb love Mary so?"
The eager children cry;
"Why, Mary loves the lamb, you know,"
The teacher did reply.

Georgie Porgie

Georgie Porgie, pudding and pie,
Kissed the girls and made them cry.
When the boys came out to play,
Georgie Porgie ran away.

Come, Follow

Come, follow, follow, follow,
Follow, follow, follow me!
Whither shall I follow, follow, follow,
Whither shall I follow, follow thee?
To the greenwood, to the greenwood,
To the greenwood, greenwood tree.

Jack Be Nimble

Jack be nimble,
Jack be quick.
Jack jump over
The candlestick.

The North Wind Doth Blow

The north wind doth blow,
And we shall have snow,
And what will poor robin do then?
Poor thing.
He'll sit in a barn,
And keep himself warm,
And hide his head under his wing,
Poor thing.

Ride a Cockhorse

Ride a cockhorse to Banbury Cross,
To see a fine lady upon a white horse.
With rings on her fingers and bells on her toes,
She shall have music wherever she goes.

To Market, to Market

To market, to market,
To buy a fat pig,
Home again, home again,
Jiggety-jig;
To market, to market,
To buy a fat hog,
Home again, home again,
Jiggety-jog.
To market, to market,
To buy a plum bun,
Home again, home again,
Market is done.

There Was an Old Woman

There was an old woman who lived in a shoe,
She had so many children she didn't know what to do.
So she gave them some broth without any bread,
And she whipped them all soundly and sent them
to bed!

The Lion and the Unicorn

The lion and the unicorn
Were fighting for the crown;
The lion beat the unicorn
All around the town.

Some gave them white bread,
And some gave them brown;
Some gave them plum cake
And drummed them out of town.

Heigh-Ho, the Carrion Crow

A carrion crow sat on an oak,
Fol-de-riddle, lol-de-riddle, hi-ding-do.
Watching a tailor shape his cloak.
Sing heigh-ho, the carrion crow,
Fol-de-riddle, lol-de-riddle, hi-ding-do.

The carrion crow began to rave,
Fol-de-riddle, lol-de-riddle, hi-ding-do.
And called the tailor a crooked knave.
Sing heigh-ho, the carrion crow,
Fol-de-riddle, lol-de-riddle, hi-ding-do.

Wife, bring me my old bent bow,
Fol-de-riddle, lol-de-riddle, hi-ding-do.
That I may shoot yon carrion crow.
Sing heigh-ho, the carrion crow,
Fol-de-riddle, lol-de-riddle, hi-ding-do.

The tailor shot and missed his mark,
Fol-de-riddle, lol-de-riddle, hi-ding-do.
And shot his own sow quite through the heart.
Sing heigh-ho, the carrion crow,
Fol-de-riddle, lol-de-riddle, hi-ding-do.

Wife, bring brandy in a spoon,
Fol-de-riddle, lol-de-riddle, hi-ding-do.
For our old sow is in a swoon.
Sing heigh-ho, the carrion crow,
Fol-de-riddle, lol-de-riddle, hi-ding-do.

Diddle, Diddle, Dumpling

Diddle, diddle, dumpling, my son John,
Went to bed with his trousers on;
One shoe off, and one shoe on,
Diddle, diddle, dumpling, my son John!

Three Children Sliding

Three children sliding on the ice,
Upon a summer's day;
As it fell out, they all fell in,
The rest they ran away.

Now had these children been at home,
Or sliding on dry ground,
Ten thousand pounds to one penny,
They had not all been drowned.

You parents that have children dear,
And you that have got none,
If you would have them safe abroad,
Pray keep them safe at home.

Two Little Dicky Birds

Two little dicky birds,
Sitting on a wall;
One named Peter,
One named Paul.
Fly away, Peter!
Fly away, Paul!
Come back, Peter!
Come back, Paul!

When the Snow Is on the Ground

The little robin grieves
When the snow is on the ground,
For the trees have no leaves,
And no berries can be found.

The air is cold, the worms are hid;
For robin here, what can be done?
Let's strow around some crumbs of bread,
And then he'll live till snow is gone.

Ding, Dong, Bell

Ding, dong, bell,
Pussy's in the well.
Who put her in?
Little Johnny Flynn.
Who pulled her out?
Little Tommy Stout.

What a naughty boy was that
To try to drown poor pussycat,
Who never did him any harm,
But killed the mice in his father's barn.

Jenny Wren

As little Jenny Wren
Was sitting by her shed.
She waggled with her tail,
And nodded with her head.
She waggled with her tail,
And nodded with her head,
As little Jenny Wren
Was sitting by the shed.

There Was an Old Lady

There was an old lady who swallowed a fly;
I don't know why she swallowed a fly —
perhaps she'll die!

There was an old lady who swallowed a spider
That wriggled and wiggled and tiggled inside her.
She swallowed the spider to catch the fly;
I don't know why she swallowed a fly —
perhaps she'll die!

There was an old lady who swallowed a bird;
How absurd to swallow a bird.
She swallowed the bird to catch the spider,
She swallowed the spider to catch the fly;
I don't know why she swallowed a fly —
perhaps she'll die!

There was an old lady who swallowed a cat;
Fancy that, to swallow a cat!
She swallowed the cat to catch the bird,
She swallowed the bird to catch the spider,
She swallowed the spider to catch the fly;
I don't know why she swallowed a fly —
perhaps she'll die!

There was an old lady who swallowed a dog;
What a hog, to swallow a dog.
She swallowed the dog to catch the cat,
She swallowed the cat to catch the bird,
She swallowed the bird to catch the spider,
She swallowed the spider to catch the fly;
I don't know why she swallowed a fly —
perhaps she'll die!

There was an old lady who swallowed a cow,
I don't know how she swallowed a cow.
She swallowed the cow to catch the dog,
She swallowed the dog to catch the cat,
She swallowed the cat to catch the bird,
She swallowed the bird to catch the spider,
She swallowed the spider to catch the fly;
I don't know why she swallowed a fly —
perhaps she'll die!

There was an old lady who swallowed
a horse . . .
She's dead, of course!

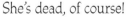

Little Tommy Tucker

Little Tommy Tucker
Sings for his supper.
What shall we give him?
White bread and butter.
How shall he cut it
Without a knife?
How shall he marry
Without a wife?

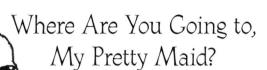

Where Are You Going to, My Pretty Maid?

"Where are you going to,
my pretty maid?"
"I'm going a-milking, sir," she said.

"May I go with you, my pretty maid?"
"You're kindly welcome, sir," she said.

"What is your father, my pretty maid?"
"My father's a farmer, sir," she said.

"Say, will you marry me, my pretty maid?"
"Yes, if you please, kind sir," she said.

"What is your fortune, my pretty maid?"
"My face is my fortune, sir," she said.

"Then I can't marry you, my pretty maid!"
"Nobody asked you, sir," she said.

Goosey, Goosey Gander

Goosey, Goosey Gander,
Where shall I wander?
Upstairs, downstairs,
And in my lady's chamber.
There I met an old man
Who wouldn't say his prayers,
I took him by the left leg
And threw him down the stairs.

Hot Cross Buns

Hot cross buns! Hot cross buns!
One a penny, two a penny,
Hot cross buns!
If you have no daughters,
Give them to your sons.
One a penny, two a penny,
Hot cross buns!

If All the Seas Were One Sea

If all the seas were one sea,
What a *great* sea that would be!
And if all the trees were one tree,
What a *great* tree that would be!
And if all the axes were one ax,
What a *great* ax that would be!
And if all the men were one man,
What a *great* man he would be!
And if the *great* man took the *great* ax,
And cut down the *great* tree
And let it fall into the *great* sea,
What a splish-splash *that* would be!

Horsey, Horsey

Horsey, horsey, don't you stop,
Just let your feet go clippetty-clop;
The tail goes swish and the wheels go 'round,
Giddy up, we're homeward bound.

Little Robin Redbreast

Little Robin Redbreast sat upon a tree,
Up went pussycat and down went he;
Down came pussycat, and away Robin ran;
Says little Robin Redbreast, "Catch me if you can."

Little Robin Redbreast jumped upon a wall,
Pussycat jumped after him and almost had a fall;
Little Robin chirped and sang, and what did pussy say?
Pussycat said, "Meow," and Robin flew away.

Ring Around the Rosie

Ring around the rosie,
A pocket full of posies,
Ashes, ashes,
We all fall down.

Pussycat, Pussycat

"Pussycat, pussycat,
Where have you been?"
"I've been up to London
To look at the queen."

"Pussycat, pussycat,
What did you there?"
"I frightened a little mouse
Under her chair."

There Was a Little Girl

There was a little girl,
Who had a little curl,
Right in the middle of her forehead.
When she was good,
She was very, very good,
But when she was bad, she was horrid.

This Is the House That Jack Built

This is the house that Jack built.

This is the malt that lay in the house that Jack built.

This is the rat that ate the malt
That lay in the house that Jack built.

This is the cat that killed the rat
That ate the malt that lay in the house that Jack built.

This is the dog that worried the cat
That killed the rat that ate the malt
That lay in the house that Jack built.

This is the cow with the crumpled horn
That tossed the dog that worried the cat
That killed the rat that ate the malt
That lay in the house that Jack built.

This is the maiden, all forlorn,
That milked the cow with the crumpled horn
That tossed the dog that worried the cat
That killed the rat that ate the malt
That lay in the house that Jack built.

This is the man, all tattered and torn,
That kissed the maiden, all forlorn,
That milked the cow with the crumpled horn
That tossed the dog that worried the cat
That killed the rat that ate the malt
That lay in the house that Jack built.

This is the priest, all shaven and shorn,
That married the man, all tattered and torn,
That kissed the maiden, all forlorn,
That milked the cow with the crumpled horn
That tossed the dog that worried the cat
That killed the rat that ate the malt
That lay in the house that Jack built.

This is the cock that crowed in the morn
That waked the priest, all shaven and shorn,
That married the man, all tattered and torn,
That kissed the maiden, all forlorn,
That milked the cow with the crumpled horn
That tossed the dog that worried the cat
That killed the rat that ate the malt
That lay in the house that Jack built.

This is the farmer, sowing his corn,
That kept the cock that crowed in the morn
That waked the priest, all shaven and shorn,
That married the man, all tattered and torn,
That kissed the maiden, all forlorn,
That milked the cow with the crumpled horn
That tossed the dog that worried the cat
That killed the rat that ate the malt
That lay in the house that Jack built!

Old Father Long-Legs

Old Father Long-Legs
Can't say his prayers.
Take him by the left leg,
And throw him down the stairs.
And when he's at the bottom,
Before he long has lain,
Take him by the right leg,
And throw him up again.

Once I Saw a Little Bird

Once I saw a little bird
Come hop, hop, hop,
And I cried, "Little bird,
Will you stop, stop, stop?"

I was going to the window
To say, "How do you do?"
But he shook his little tail
And away he flew.

Little Boy Blue

Little Boy Blue,
Come blow your horn,
The sheep's in the meadow,
The cow's in the corn;
But where's the boy
Who looks after the sheep?
"He's under a haystack
Fast asleep."
Will you wake him?
"No, not I,
For if I do,
He's sure to cry."

Curly Locks

Curly Locks, Curly Locks,
Wilt thou be mine?
Thou shalt not wash dishes
Nor yet feed the swine,
But sit on a cushion
And sew a fine seam,
And feed upon strawberries,
Sugar, and cream.

I Had a Little Pony

I had a little pony,
His name was Dapple Gray;
I lent him to a lady
To ride a mile away.

She whipped him, she slashed him,
She rode him through the mire;
I would not lend my pony now,
For all the lady's hire.

One, Two, Buckle My Shoe

One, two,
Buckle my shoe;
Three, four,
Knock at the door;
Five, six,
Pick up sticks;
Seven, eight,
Lay them straight;
Nine, ten,
A big fat hen;
Eleven, twelve,
Dig and delve;
Thirteen, fourteen,
Maids a-courting;
Fifteen, sixteen,
Maids in the kitchen;
Seventeen, eighteen,
Maids in waiting;
Nineteen, twenty,
My plate's empty.

One, Two, Three, Four, Five

One, two, three, four, five,
Once I caught a fish alive,
Six, seven, eight, nine, ten,
Then I let it go again.

Why did you let it go?
Because it bit my finger so.
Which finger did it bite?
This little finger on the right.

Cry Baby Bunting

Cry Baby Bunting,
Daddy's gone a-hunting.
Gone to fetch a rabbit skin,
To wrap the Baby Bunting in.
Cry Baby Bunting.

Solomon Grundy

Solomon Grundy,
Born on a Monday,
Christened on Tuesday,
Married on Wednesday,
Took ill on Thursday,
Worse on Friday,
Died on Saturday,
Buried on Sunday.
This is the end of
Solomon Grundy.

Whistle

"Whistle, daughter, whistle,
Whistle, daughter dear."

"I cannot whistle, Mammy,
I cannot whistle clear."

"Whistle, daughter, whistle,
Whistle for a pound."

"I cannot whistle, Mammy,
I cannot make a sound."

Dame Trot and Her Cat

Dame Trot and her cat
Led a peaceable life,
When they were not troubled
With other folks' strife.

When Dame had her dinner,
Pussy would wait
And was sure to receive
A nice piece from her plate.

Boys and Girls
Come Out to Play

Boys and girls come out to play,
The moon doth shine as bright as day.
Leave your supper and leave your sleep,
And join your playfellows in the street.
Come with a whoop and come with a call,
Come with a good will or not at all.

Up the ladder and down the wall,
A halfpenny loaf will serve us all;
You find milk, and I'll find flour,
And we'll have a pudding in half
an hour.

Three Little Kittens

Three little kittens, they lost their mittens,
And they began to cry,
"Oh, Mother dear, we sadly fear
That we have lost our mittens."
"What? Lost your mittens, you naughty kittens!
Then you shall have no pie."
"Mee-ow, mee-ow, mee-ow.
Now we shall have no pie."

The three little kittens, they found their mittens,
And they began to cry,
"Oh, Mother dear, see here, see here,
For we have found our mittens."
"What? Found your mittens, you silly kittens,
Then you shall have some pie."
"Mee-ow, mee-ow, mee-ow,
Oh, let us have some pie."

The three little kittens put on their mittens,
And soon ate up the pie.
"Oh, Mother dear, we greatly fear
That we have soiled our mittens."
"What? Soiled your mittens, you naughty kittens!"
Then they began to sigh,
"Mee-ow, mee-ow, mee-ow."
Then they began to sigh.

The three little kittens, they washed their mittens,
And hung them out to dry.
"Oh, Mother dear, look here, look here,
We have washed our mittens."
"What? Washed your mittens, you're good little kittens,
But I smell a rat close by."
"Mee-ow, mee-ow, mee-ow.
We smell a rat close by."

Twinkle, Twinkle, Little Star

Twinkle, twinkle, little star,
How I wonder what you are!
Up above the world so high,
Like a diamond in the sky.

When the blazing sun is gone,
When he nothing shines upon,
Then you show your little light,
Twinkle, twinkle, all the night.

Then the traveler in the dark,
Thanks you for your tiny spark,
He could not see which way to go
If you did not twinkle so.

In the dark blue sky you keep,
And often through my curtains peep,
For you never shut your eye
Till the sun is in the sky.

As your bright and tiny spark,
Lights the traveler in the dark,
Though I know not what you are,
Twinkle, twinkle, little star.

Three Blind Mice

Three blind mice, three blind mice,
See how they run, see how they run.
They all ran after the farmer's wife,
Who cut off their tails with a carving knife.
Did you ever see such a thing in your life,
As three blind mice?

The Cocks Crow

The cocks crow in the morn
To tell us to rise,
And he that lies late
Will never be wise.
For early to bed,
And early to rise,
Is the way to be healthy
And wealthy and wise.

Rub-A-Dub-Dub

Rub-a-dub-dub,
Three men in a tub,
And how do you think they got there?
The butcher, the baker,
The candlestick maker,
They all jumped out of a rotten potato,
'Twas enough to make a man stare.

Hark, Hark, the Dogs Do Bark

Hark, hark,
The dogs do bark,
The beggars are coming to town.
Some in rags,
And some in jags,
And one in a velvet gown.

Little Miss Muffet

Little Miss Muffet
Sat on a tuffet,
Eating her curds and whey;
Along came a spider,
Who sat down beside her
And frightened Miss Muffet away.

Simple Simon

Simple Simon met a pieman,
Going to the fair;
Said Simple Simon to the pieman,
"Let me taste your ware."

Said the pieman to Simple Simon,
"Show me first your penny."
Said Simple Simon to the pieman,
"Indeed, I have not any!"

Simple Simon went a-fishing,
For to catch a whale;
All the water he had got
Was in his mother's pail.

Simple Simon went to look
If plums grew on a thistle;
He pricked his fingers very much,
Which made poor Simon whistle.

He went for water in a sieve,
But soon it all fell through;
And now poor Simple Simon
Bids you all, "Adieu."

To Bed, to Bed

"To bed, to bed," says Sleepyhead;
"Tarry awhile," says Slow;
"Put on the pan," says Greedy Nan,
"We'll sup before we go."

Higgledy, Piggledy, My Black Hen

Higgledy, piggledy, my black hen,
She lays eggs for gentlemen;
Sometimes nine, and sometimes ten;
Higgledy, piggledy, my black hen.

Wee Willie Winkie

Wee Willie Winkie runs through the town,
Upstairs and downstairs in his nightgown,
Tapping at the window and crying through the lock,
"Are all the children in their beds? Now it's eight o'clock."

Pat-A-Cake,
Pat-A-Cake

Pat-a-cake, pat-a-cake, baker's man,
Bake me a cake as fast as you can;
Pat it and prick it and mark it with "B,"
And put it in the oven for Baby and me.

This Little Piggy

This little piggy went to market,
This little piggy stayed at home,
This little piggy had roast beef,
This little piggy had none.
And this little piggy went,
"Wee, wee, wee," all the way home.

Polly, Put the Kettle On

Polly, put the kettle on,
Polly, put the kettle on,
Polly, put the kettle on,
We'll all have tea.

Sukey, take it off again,
Sukey, take it off again,
Sukey, take it off again,
They've all gone away.

There Was a Crooked Man

There was a crooked man and he walked a crooked mile;
He found a crooked sixpence upon a crooked stile;
He bought a crooked cat, which caught a crooked mouse,
And they all lived together in a little crooked house.

Little Jack Horner

Little Jack Horner
Sat in the corner,
Eating a Christmas pie;
He put in his thumb
And pulled out a plum,
And said, "What a good boy am I!"

Monday's Child

Monday's child is fair of face,
Tuesday's child is full of grace,
Wednesday's child is full of woe,
Thursday's child has far to go,
Friday's child is loving and giving,
Saturday's child works hard for his living,
And the child that is born on the Sabbath day
Is bonny and blithe, and good and gay.

Doctor Foster

Doctor Foster went to Gloucester
In a shower of rain;
He stepped in a puddle,
Right up to his middle,
And never went there again!

If you liked **The Nursery Rhyme Book,** you'll love **The Games Book!**

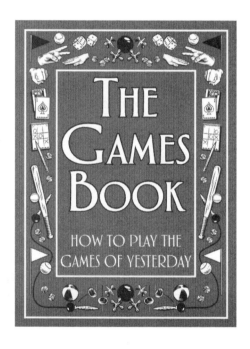

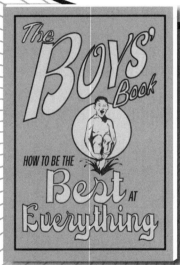

Treat your family to something AMAZING!

The Family Book

AMAZING THINGS TO DO TOGETHER

- OPTICAL ILLUSIONS AND MAGIC TRICKS
- MIND-BOGGLING PUZZLES AND RIDDLES
- UNIQUE ARTS AND CRAFTS

And more!